BUG WARS

Written by Steve Parker

Illustrated by Simon Mendez

Ticktock

An Hachette UK Company
www.hachette.co.uk

First published in the USA in 2014 by Ticktock,
an imprint of Octopus Publishing Group Ltd
Endeavour House
189 Shaftesbury Avenue
London
WC2H 8JY
www.octopusbooks.co.uk
www.octopusbooksusa.com
www.ticktockbooks.com

Distributed in the US by
Hachette Book Group USA
237 Park Avenue
New York, NY 10017, USA

Distributed in Canada by
Canadian Manda Group
165 Dufferin Street
Toronto, Ontario, Canada M6K 3H6

ISBN 978 1 78325 146 9

Printed and bound in China
1 3 5 7 9 10 8 6 4 2

Project Editor Carey Scott
Design Perfect Bound Ltd and Leah Germann
Publisher Samantha Sweeney
Commissioning Editor Anna Bowles
Managing Editor Karen Rigden
Editorial Assistant Phoebe Morgan
Production Controller Sarah Connelly
US Editor Jennifer Dixon

Picture Credits

CONTENTS

AWESOME PICTURES!
SO REAL YOU'LL THINK THEY'RE PHOTOS!

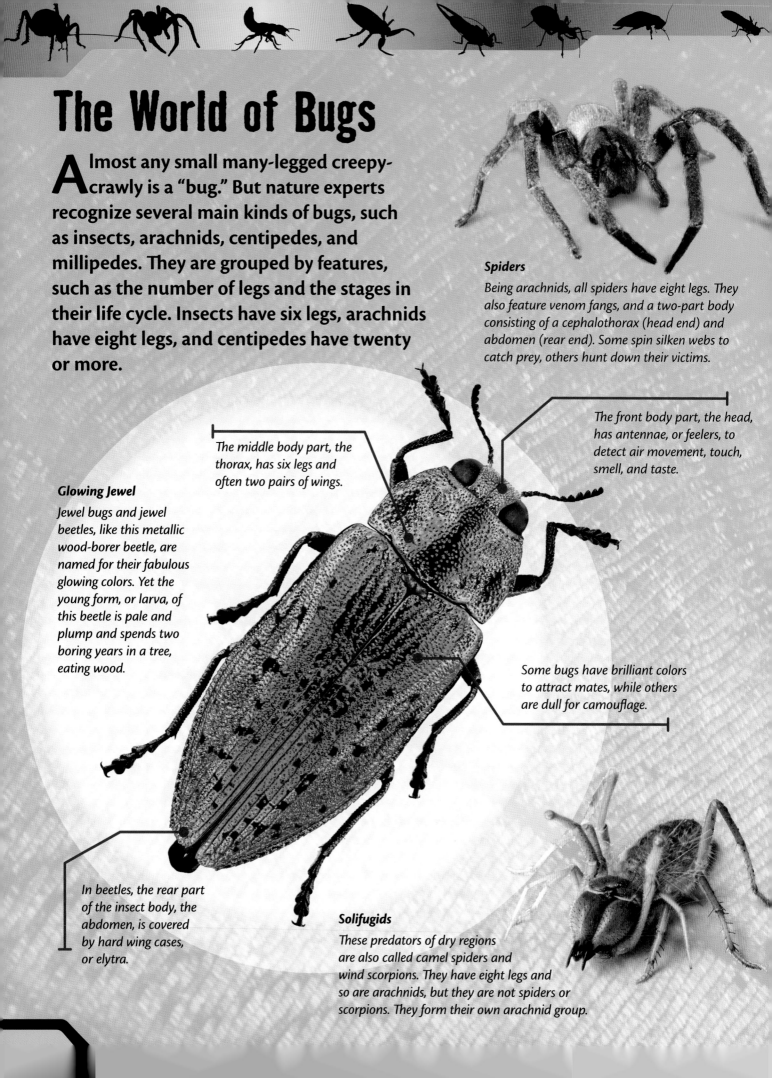

The World of Bugs

Almost any small many-legged creepy-crawly is a "bug." But nature experts recognize several main kinds of bugs, such as insects, arachnids, centipedes, and millipedes. They are grouped by features, such as the number of legs and the stages in their life cycle. Insects have six legs, arachnids have eight legs, and centipedes have twenty or more.

Spiders

Being arachnids, all spiders have eight legs. They also feature venom fangs, and a two-part body consisting of a cephalothorax (head end) and abdomen (rear end). Some spin silken webs to catch prey, others hunt down their victims.

The front body part, the head, has antennae, or feelers, to detect air movement, touch, smell, and taste.

The middle body part, the thorax, has six legs and often two pairs of wings.

Glowing Jewel

Jewel bugs and jewel beetles, like this metallic wood-borer beetle, are named for their fabulous glowing colors. Yet the young form, or larva, of this beetle is pale and plump and spends two boring years in a tree, eating wood.

Some bugs have brilliant colors to attract mates, while others are dull for camouflage.

In beetles, the rear part of the insect body, the abdomen, is covered by hard wing cases, or elytra.

Solifugids

These predators of dry regions are also called camel spiders and wind scorpions. They have eight legs and so are arachnids, but they are not spiders or scorpions. They form their own arachnid group.

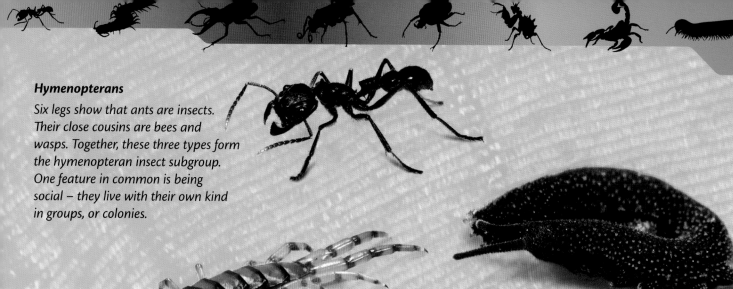

Hymenopterans

Six legs show that ants are insects. Their close cousins are bees and wasps. Together, these three types form the hymenopteran insect subgroup. One feature in common is being social – they live with their own kind in groups, or colonies.

Onychophorans

Among the strangest and most mysterious of all bugs, velvet worms seem to be an odd mix of several other creatures. They have their own group, the onychophorans, which seems to have no close relatives.

Chilopods

Their name means "100 legs" but most centipedes have between 20 and 60, although a few have over 250. They also have long fanglike venom claws at the front end! They make up their own bug group, the chilopods.

Mantises

The preying mantis seems to have four legs and two fearsome grabbing pincers. But the pincers are really its front legs, so the mantis is an insect. It is one of the toughest and fastest of all bugs – a wonderfully designed killer!

Bug Life Cycles

Almost all kinds of bugs begin life as eggs laid by an adult female. Some newly hatched baby bugs look like their parents, and shed their skin several times as they grow larger. Other baby bugs look very different to the adult and go through one or more shape changes known as metamorphosis.

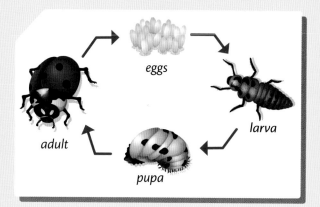

eggs

larva

pupa

adult

Ladybug life cycle

egg

Nymph to adult

Bed bug life cycle

Battling Bugs

Enter the fearsome world of bugs, where gruesome behavior occurs every day. But what would happen if the most awesome of bugs were to meet outside their natural habitats? Using incredible computer-generated illustrations, this book creates amazing scenes and bugs so real that you'll think they're photographs!

The beetle has very hard protective wing covers over its main body.

AWESOME PICTURES

So real you'll think they're photos!

Warfare and Weapons

Most bugs have a hard outer body casing called an exoskeleton, which is difficult to penetrate. As the Goliath beetle and giant weta grapple, each searches for a soft spot or vulnerable part, such as the eye or antenna.

A possible soft spot is one of the joints in the leg.

Most bugs have clawed feet to scratch and rip.

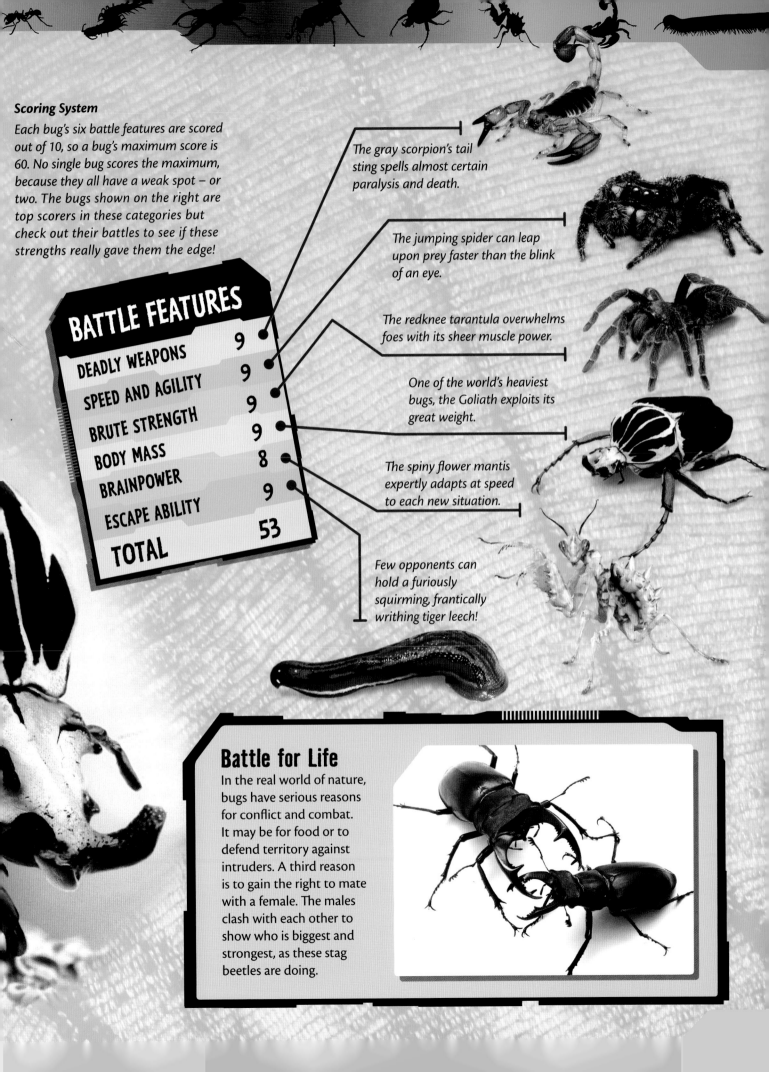

Scoring System

Each bug's six battle features are scored out of 10, so a bug's maximum score is 60. No single bug scores the maximum, because they all have a weak spot – or two. The bugs shown on the right are top scorers in these categories but check out their battles to see if these strengths really gave them the edge!

BATTLE FEATURES

DEADLY WEAPONS	9
SPEED AND AGILITY	9
BRUTE STRENGTH	9
BODY MASS	9
BRAINPOWER	8
ESCAPE ABILITY	9
TOTAL	**53**

The gray scorpion's tail sting spells almost certain paralysis and death.

The jumping spider can leap upon prey faster than the blink of an eye.

The redknee tarantula overwhelms foes with its sheer muscle power.

One of the world's heaviest bugs, the Goliath exploits its great weight.

The spiny flower mantis expertly adapts at speed to each new situation.

Few opponents can hold a furiously squirming, frantically writhing tiger leech!

Battle for Life

In the real world of nature, bugs have serious reasons for conflict and combat. It may be for food or to defend territory against intruders. A third reason is to gain the right to mate with a female. The males clash with each other to show who is biggest and strongest, as these stag beetles are doing.

Tail-raising Clash

It's a stand-off – or rather, a tail-off. A foraging devil's coach horse beetle detects the scent of an easy meal, in the shape of a bug's nest of eggs. But the devil reckoned without the eggs' mother – a giant earwig. Unusual for an insect, she protects her brood with a ferocious fight back. Menacing in black, the beetle waves its powerful head, clacks its scissorlike mandibles, and curls its tail – ready to spray a stinking fluid. The earwig, smooth and slinky, also raises her rear end to display its pincer endings. These can nip hard, but they can't deal out death – but does the devil beetle know that?

GIANT EARWIG

Scientific name: *Titanolabis*
How to say it: *Tie-tan-owe-lab-iss*

CREATURE FEATURE

Cerci, pincerlike tail prongs that can grab but not crush with power

BATTLE FEATURES

DEADLY WEAPONS	7
SPEED AND AGILITY	8
BRUTE STRENGTH	6
BODY MASS	4
BRAINPOWER	5
ESCAPE ABILITY	8
TOTAL	**38**

A member of the insect group called dermapterans ("**skin-wings**"), the earwig is usually a peaceful creature. With its medium-sized mouthparts, it hunts smaller bugs such as termites and munches on bits of old plants, leaves, and fruits, but it cannot deliver a large or venomous bite. Its main weapons are the long **pincerlike cerci** at the tail end, used to grab and hold, and its ability to bend and wriggle at great speed during **attack and escape**.

COVERED BACK

Beetles have four wings – sort of! The front two, called elytra, are covers that protect the larger, delicate hindwings. For flight, the elytra hinge up to reveal the hindwings, which then fold out for flapping.

Cerci are fairly sharp, sometimes used to stab

Flattened, bendy body capable of fast movement

Leathery front wings, or forewings, are hard and tough

LENGTH 1.2 in. (30 mm)

DEVIL'S COACH HORSE BEETLE

Scientific name: *Ocypus*
How to say it: *Oh-sigh-puss*

BATTLE FEATURES

DEADLY WEAPONS	7
BRUTE STRENGTH	6
BODY MASS	5
BRAINPOWER	6
TOTAL	**35**

Beetles, or **coleopterans** ("**covered wings**"), are by far the biggest insect group, with over 400,000 different species. The devil's coach horse, named for its **devilish black color**, is a **rove beetle**, or **staphylinid**, always searching for small prey such as worms, ants, and baby slugs. The strong mandibles (jaws) are set onto a large powerful head. Its habit of bending up its rear body like a scorpion warns that it can emit a **foul odor** from its back end.

CREATURE FEATURE

Glands at tail end emit fluid that smells awful and tastes terrible!

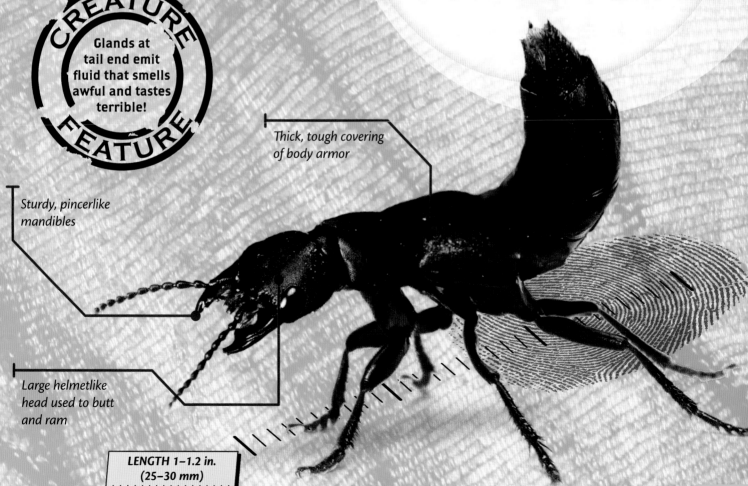

Thick, tough covering of body armor

Sturdy, pincerlike mandibles

Large helmetlike head used to butt and ram

LENGTH 1–1.2 in.
(25–30 mm)

Fangs against Stings

Death has never been so close, as two champions of venom grapple for an advantage. The Brazilian wandering spider's legs are striving to hold the hornet's wings as it maneuvers its fangs to stab the hornet's soft abdomen – the head and thorax are reinforced against attack. The giant hornet attempts to avoid the fatal fangs as it twists its tail stinger around to impale the spider, while also trying to snip off one of its legs with sharp mandibles. Such is the might of their chemical weapons! Each knows that whoever lands the first venom will secure victory.

BRAZILIAN WANDERING SPIDER

Scientific name: *Phoneutria*
How to say it: *Foe-new-tree-ah*

One of the world's **deadliest** spiders, the Brazilian wandering spider is of course not an insect. It's a member of the **lycosid** or **"wolf" arachnid** group, which prowl at night rather than making webs or nests. It's not quite the biggest spider species, but it has a great set of **attack weapons** – large fangs, extremely powerful venom, and fast reactions. It can move **like lightning** on its long strong legs and **strike with its bite** in the blink of an eye.

BATTLE FEATURES

DEADLY WEAPONS	9
SPEED AND AGILITY	8
BRUTE STRENGTH	8
BODY MASS	8
BRAINPOWER	6
ESCAPE ABILITY	8
TOTAL	**47**

CREATURE FEATURE

Large fangs deliver exceptionally strong venom

Hair on body and legs can irritate an attacker

Eight eyes detect the slightest movement of predator or prey

Long, strong, fast-moving legs

LENGTH 0.7–1.9 in. (17–48 mm)
LEGS up to 6 in. (150 mm)

GIANT HORNET

Scientific name: *Vespa mandarinia*
How to say it: *Vess-pah man-dah-reen-ee-ah*

BATTLE FEATURES

DEADLY WEAPONS	8
SPEED AND AGILITY	7
BRUTE STRENGTH	8
BODY MASS	7
BRAINPOWER	6
ESCAPE ABILITY	8
TOTAL	44

CREATURE FEATURE

Long, sharp, stiff stinger injects really painful venom

A huge version of the common wasp, the giant hornet is in the **Hymenoptera,** or "**membrane wing,**" insect group, along with bees, ants, and sawflies. The giant hornet has a very large and very **deadly rear stinger**. As in other wasps, and unlike bees, this stinger is smooth rather than barbed or hooked, so it can sting repeatedly. This beast is an **out-and-out hunter,** killing other even bigger bugs as food for itself and for its own larvae (grubs).

HIVE-BOMBER

The giant hornet loves to lay waste to honeybee hives. It kills at speed, chopping off the bees' heads at the rate of one every two seconds. This is a form of self-protection from the bees' suicide stings. The attack also provides food, both as dead bee bodies and the now-unprotected grubs, which the hornet eats or carries away to its own nest for its young.

Sharp mandibles (jaws) easily slice up even hard-cased prey

Strong wings for fast, powerful flight

Yellow and black warning colors for venom

LENGTH 2 in. (50 mm)
WINGSPAN 3 in. (76 mm)

Brawn against Bravery

Scrambling slowly along a branch, the Madagascar hissing cockroach is suddenly surprised by a lightning strike from a spiny flower mantis. The mantis, away from its usual flower home, was also surprised and so struck first, slashing out with its spiky, shearing forelegs in the hope of slicing off the cockroach's delicate antennae or piercing its vulnerable eyes. With size and weight on its side, the 'roach hisses loudly and kicks wildly at the mantis with its clawed feet, trying to disable its forelegs or tear open its huge all-seeing eyes.

SPINY FLOWER MANTIS

Scientific name: *Pseudocreobotra wahlbergii*
How to say it: *Sude-oh-kree-oh-bot-rah wall-berg-ee-eye*

BATTLE FEATURES

DEADLY WEAPONS	8
SPEED AND AGILITY	9
BRUTE STRENGTH	7
BODY MASS	7
BRAINPOWER	8
ESCAPE ABILITY	8
TOTAL	**47**

Members of the mantis insect group are called **mantodeans**, or "**prophet shapes**," after their "praying" posture – the front legs held up as though with hands together. For their size, they are among the bug kingdom's most **efficient killing machines**, with incredibly fast reactions. The spiny flower mantis is one of the sneakiest, lurking well camouflaged to snap up almost any prey that visits its flower.

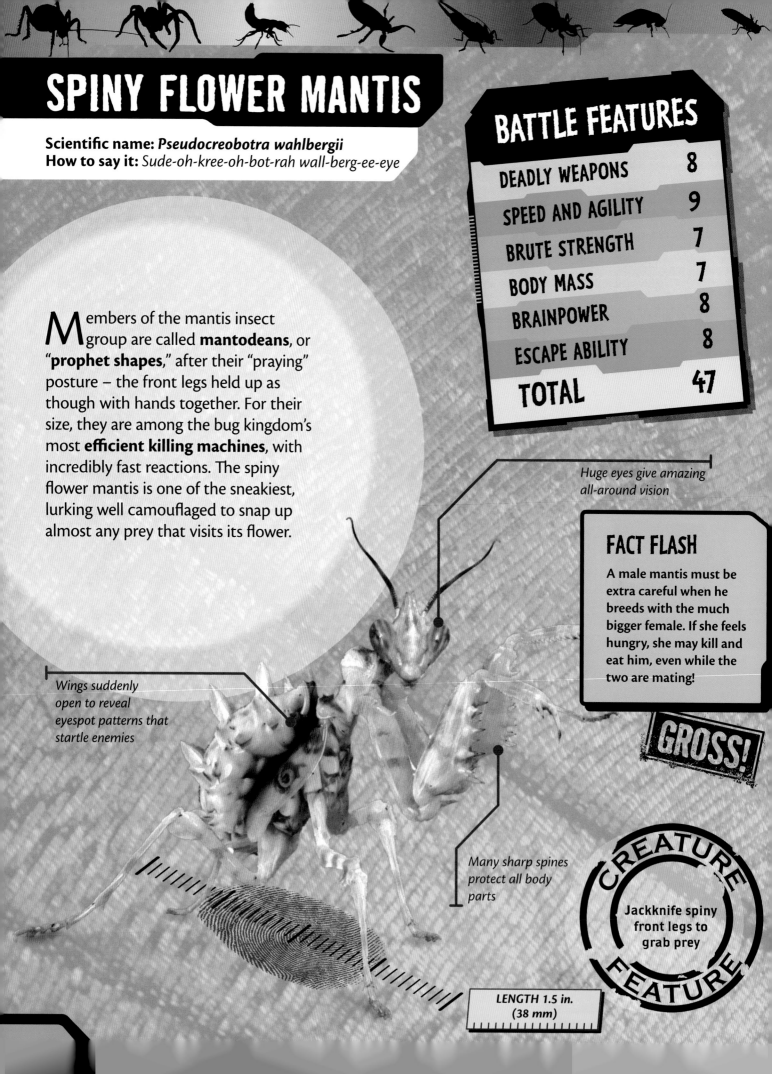

Huge eyes give amazing all-around vision

FACT FLASH

A male mantis must be extra careful when he breeds with the much bigger female. If she feels hungry, she may kill and eat him, even while the two are mating!

GROSS!

Wings suddenly open to reveal eyespot patterns that startle enemies

Many sharp spines protect all body parts

CREATURE FEATURE
Jackknife spiny front legs to grab prey

LENGTH 1.5 in. (38 mm)

MADAGASCAR HISSING COCKROACH

Scientific name: *Gromphadorhina portentosa*
How to say it: *Grom-fad-or-reen-ah poor-tent-owe-sah*

BATTLE FEATURES

DEADLY WEAPONS	6
SPEED AND AGILITY	5
BRUTE STRENGTH	8
BODY MASS	8
BRAINPOWER	6
ESCAPE ABILITY	5
TOTAL	**38**

CREATURE FEATURE

Loud hiss made by blowing air out of breathing holes (spiracles) along sides of body

The Madagascar hissing cockroach belongs to the cockroach group of bugs, **blattodeans** ("**common insects**"). It does not have venom or poison and it lacks massive strong jaws, but it is big, bulky, sturdy, and strong. The male has bumplike "horns" called **tubercles**, usually used to ram rival males at breeding time, or to repel enemies. Like most other cockroaches, the **hisser** eats mainly bits of fruits, seeds, and other plant matter.

Thick, leathery body covering prevents injuries

Front "horns" push and shove away enemies

Spiky legs can deliver a colossal kick

**LENGTH 2–3 in.
(50–75 mm)**

Armor-piercing Soldiers

With no thought for their own survival, soldier termites rush into a mass attack on their nest intruder. The giant millipede, usually slow and inoffensive, has accidentally wandered into their domain. Is the multileg about to pay with its life? The soldiers' outsized jaws, as big as their heads, are like bug can-openers trying to slice through the millipede's tough outer casing. The 'pede twirls and shakes to hurl them off, and deploys a stinging irritant chemical that oozes from pores along its body, making the termites writhe in agony.

AFRICAN TERMITE

Scientific name: *Macrotermes bellicosus*
How to say it: *Mack-roe-term-eez bell-ee-koe-suss*

Termites are sometimes called white ants but they belong to a different insect group, the **isopterans**, or **"equal wings."** One worker termite – small, soft, pale, and almost defenseless – is easy prey. But a whole army of **soldier termites** is a very different prospect. Some have **mandibles**, or **jaws**, **so large** they cannot eat for themselves and have to be fed by the workers in the nest.

BATTLE FEATURES

DEADLY WEAPONS	7
SPEED AND AGILITY	6
BRUTE STRENGTH	6
BODY MASS	4
BRAINPOWER	5
ESCAPE ABILITY	6
TOTAL	**34**

Head has a thick, helmetlike covering

CREATURE FEATURE
Outsized jaws, or mandibles, sometimes bigger than the head

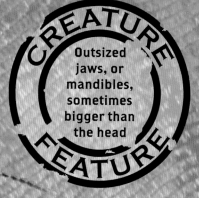

Head opening releases sticky fluid to trap enemies

Strong legs for fast movement

LENGTH 1.6 in. (40 mm)

MASS ATTACK FOR NEST DEFENSE

A large termite mound, or nest, may contain more than a million individuals. Most are busy workers. One or a few are egg-laying queens – which can live for over 40 years! The photo shows how the soldier termites stand guard at the nest openings and watch over the workers. At the first sign of trouble, the soldiers swarm over the enemy in their thousands, biting with their massive, pincerlike mandibles.

GIANT AFRICAN MILLIPEDE

Scientific name: _Archispirostreptus gigas_
How to say it: _Ark-ee-spy-roe-strep-tus gee-gas_

BATTLE FEATURES

DEADLY WEAPONS	6
SPEED AND AGILITY	7
BRUTE STRENGTH	8
BODY MASS	8
BRAINPOWER	7
ESCAPE ABILITY	8
TOTAL	**44**

CREATURE FEATURE

Produces noxious foul-tasting and awful-smelling liquid from pores along the body

Millipedes, or diplopods ("**twin paired feet**"), along with centipedes, insects, spiders, and scorpions, as well as crustaceans such as crabs, all belong to the giant animal group known as the **arthropods**, or **"jointed legs."** The giant millipede is usually a slow, harmless creature that feeds on rotting bits and pieces, such as old leaves, decaying wood, and moldy fruits. But it is well able to defend itself by writhing and **oozing foul fluids**.

GROSS!

Curls up to defend itself, protecting legs and underside

Tough body casing with overlapping joints

About 250 legs, two pairs per body segment (section)

**LENGTH 15 in.
(380 mm)**

Fatal for One

Locked in a terminal embrace, the scorpion and stag beetle tussle for advantage. The scorpion grapples and stabs with its pair of crablike pincers. The stag's antennae reach out to sense its enemy's position, better to grab the whole scorpion in its massive antlerlike mandibles. These can grip – but their muscles are not strong enough for a fatal crush. The scorpion has yet to employ its ultimate weapon and inject its deadly venom with a flick of its tail sting. Yet even if it does, can the sting penetrate the stag's armor?

STAG BEETLE

Scientific name: *Lucanus cervus*
How to say it: *Loo-can-uss ser-vuss*

BATTLE FEATURES

DEADLY WEAPONS	6
SPEED AND AGILITY	4
BRUTE STRENGTH	8
BODY MASS	8
BRAINPOWER	7
ESCAPE ABILITY	5
TOTAL	38

The male stag beetle has a long, boring start in life. It lives as a grub for up to six years, boring or tunneling in trees and eating the wood. When it finally reaches adulthood, it flies around clumsily, looking for a female for breeding. Stag beetles make up a huge family, **lucanids**, with more than 1,200 different kinds. Most are harmless, lapping up plant sap and flower nectar.

CREATURE FEATURE

Male has massive mandibles, or jaws, like a deer's antlers

Strong wing covers protect delicate flying wings

Long powerful legs end in sharp claws

Large head houses mandible-moving muscles

LENGTH 1.4–2.2 in. (35–55 mm)

FACT FLASH

The male's "antler" jaws (mandibles) are too huge and heavy to bite hard. It's the female, with much smaller jaws but quite large jaw-closing muscles, that can give a really nasty nip!

GRAY SCORPION

Scientific name: *Euscorpius flavicaudis*
How to say it: *You-score-pea-uss flav-ee-cod-iss*

BATTLE FEATURES

DEADLY WEAPONS	9
SPEED AND AGILITY	8
BRUTE STRENGTH	6
BODY MASS	5
BRAINPOWER	6
ESCAPE ABILITY	8
TOTAL	**42**

Scorpions have eight legs – so they are **arachnids**. They have their own group, **Scorpiones**, and are close cousins of spiders, mites, and ticks. Mostly **nighttime hunters**, they prowl and feel their way to locate prey such as small bugs, worms, and other creepy-crawlies. The scorpion seizes and subdues its victim in its **large pincers** and rips off pieces to digest using its **sharp, powerful mouthparts**, called chelicerae.

CREATURE FEATURE

Venomous stinger at end of tail

Tail curves and arches to position stinger over the head

Pincers (chelae) grab and tear up prey

Four pairs of legs for fast running

LENGTH 1.4–1.8 in.
(35–45 mm)

Superfast Strike

The jumping spider never leaps onto its victim without securing a length of thread as an emergency lifeline. But the masked hunter assassin bug is too quick. As the spider lands and readies its pointed fangs, the bug rips through the thread and prepares to spear its long, curved, sharp-tipped beak into the spider's soft neck area. Yet the spider has lightning speed, too. It flips the hunter over to expose its softer underbelly, once again poised to strike. Each bug stabs and jabs in a blur of fangs and beak, attempting to land the fatal hit.

MASKED HUNTER ASSASSIN BUG

Scientific name: *Reduvius personatus*
How to say it: *Ree-doo-vee-us purr-son-ah-tus*

BATTLE FEATURES

DEADLY WEAPONS	7
SPEED AND AGILITY	8
BRUTE STRENGTH	5
BODY MASS	5
BRAINPOWER	7
ESCAPE ABILITY	8
TOTAL	40

In everyday use, "bug" refers to almost any creepy-crawly, but insect experts use the word to mean a **hemipteran** ("half-wing") insect, or "true bug" (see page 36). The hemipterans have **long, sharp, piercing mouthparts**, the beak (rostrum), to stab into food and suck out the juices. For assassin bugs, the food is usually a small insect, worm, millipede, or similar prey. The assassin can also defend itself by **beak-stabbing bigger enemies**, which to humans feels like a sharp and painful bee sting.

CREATURE FEATURE

Long, snoutlike piercing "beak"

Wings for quick getaway

Large eyes for good vision

Slim but strong hairy legs

LENGTH 0.7–0.9 in. (17–22 mm)

JUMPING SPIDER

Scientific name: *Phidippus audax*
How to say it: *Fye-dip-puss aw-dacks*

CREATURE FEATURE

Main pair of large forward-facing eyes see well and judge distances precisely

SPIDER-HUNTING SPIDER!

Jumping spiders can creep onto another spider's web and mimic the struggling movements of a caught fly. When the web owner approaches, the jumper suddenly leaps onto it and deals it a deadly venomous strike.

Jumping spiders form the **salticid** ("leaping") family of spiders, with over 5,000 different species. Like other spiders, they spin silk threads, but they use these as "**lifelines**." The jumper regularly attaches its lines to firm objects and lets them trail behind as it roams around, looking for prey to stalk, leap on, and bite with **venomous fangs**. If the spider misses its target, it relies on its lifeline to work as a bungee cord and save it from a deadly fall.

Colorful hairs may have rainbowlike (iridescent) sheen

Three pairs of smaller eyes

Sharp fangs inject venom

Strong legs capable of great leaps

LENGTH 0.7–0.9 in.
(17–22 mm)

Lakeside Brawl

Amegarian banded centipede prowls along the lakeside, fast and fierce, ready to bite any small prey with its venomous, clawlike front legs. Without warning, from the water dashes its worst nightmare – a giant water bug. Long, strong, hook-tipped front legs extended to grab the enemy, the bug knows its beaklike mouthparts can inject toxic enzymes to paralyze and predigest. However the centipede is also confident in its front-end weapons, and its skills at twisting and darting in a flash to gain the upper hand – or legs. The two face up, then...

Strength or Slink?

Without warning, the giant water bug lunges forward to grab the banded centipede in its foreleg pincers, desperate to pierce its tough outer casing somewhere along the bendy body. With a lightning turn the 'pede flicks around to confront the bug and bring its venom claws into play, aiming for a daggerlike stab into the small, soft-lined joint between the bug's head and thorax. The two wrestle, the bug hard-armored but slower and stiff-moving, the centipede a superslinky wriggler so hard to pin down.

GIANT AMERICAN WATER BUG

Scientific name: *Lethocerus americanus*
How to say it: *Leth-owe-sir-uss ah-merry-can-uss*

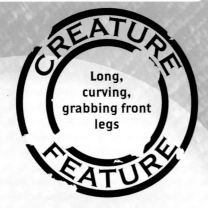

CREATURE FEATURE

Long, curving, grabbing front legs

BATTLE FEATURES

DEADLY WEAPONS	8
SPEED AND AGILITY	8
BRUTE STRENGTH	8
BODY MASS	8
BRAINPOWER	7
ESCAPE ABILITY	6
TOTAL	**45**

True bugs are the **hemipteran** group of insects (see page 30), with over 80,000 different kinds. Herbivorous hemipterans suck plant juices. Hunting types like the giant water bug dribble **toxic digesting saliva** through piercing mouthparts into their victims and suck up the soupy results. Many kinds can stay underwater while breathing by a snorkel-like air tube sticking from the rear end.

GROSS!

ATTACK OF THE TOE-BITER

- The giant water bug is a big brute of an insect and people who paddle in fresh water call it the "toe-biter" for good reason.
- Another nickname is "electric-light bug" because it flies towards lights in the darkness.

Breathing tube at rear end

Big wings for strong flight

Rear legs deliver a slashing kick

Piercing mouthparts

LENGTH 4 in.
(100 mm)

MEGARIAN BANDED CENTIPEDE

Scientific name: *Scolopendra cingulata*
How to say it: *Skoll-owe-pen-drah sin-gu-lah-tah*

BATTLE FEATURES

DEADLY WEAPONS	8
SPEED AND AGILITY	8
BRUTE STRENGTH	8
BODY MASS	8
BRAINPOWER	8
ESCAPE ABILITY	8
TOTAL	**48**

CREATURE FEATURE

Powerful venom "fangs" are claw-tipped, pincerlike front legs

Centipedes make up the group known as **chilopods**, a name that means "**lip-foot**." They are relatives of the millipedes but differ in two main ways. One is that centipedes have only two legs per body segment (section), not four. The other difference is that centipedes are fast, **fierce carnivores**, hunting prey to stab with their venomous "fangs," known as forcipules, which are in fact their front pair of legs, each ending in a **toothlike, piercing claw.**

Two legs per body segment

Antennae sense surroundings

Flexible, fast-moving body

LENGTH 4–6 in.
(100–150 mm)

Living Larder

It's an epic encounter between two old enemies that have clashed so often through evolutionary time. The tarantula hawk wasp feeds inoffensively on nectar and pollen – but it is driven to thrust its venomous tail stinger into the tarantula, to paralyze it as a living larder for its grubs. The spider counters by rearing up in typical tarantula fashion, front legs aiming to kick the wasp, long dripping fangs prepared to assault, and rear legs kicking showers of irritant hairs onto the wasp's head and eyes. Both know the first thrust will be the last.

TARANTULA HAWK WASP

Scientific name: *Pepsis formosa*
How to say it: *Pep-siss form-oh-sah*

CREATURE FEATURE

Sharp, stiff, multi-use tail stinger injects intense venom

BATTLE FEATURES

DEADLY WEAPONS	8
SPEED AND AGILITY	7
BRUTE STRENGTH	8
BODY MASS	7
BRAINPOWER	5
ESCAPE ABILITY	7
TOTAL	**42**

Wasps, along with sawflies, bees, and ants, belong to the giant insect group called **hymenopterans**, or "**sheet wings**," with over 150,000 species. Hawk wasps are named because they hunt like hawks, circling to find a victim and then diving onto it, to grapple and inject the **fearsome sting** before the surprised victim reacts. Unlike a bee's sting, the wasp's lacks barbs, so it can stab again and again.

GROSS!

SPIDER-SLAYER

The tarantula hawk wasp paralyzes a tarantula or similar spider with its venom, takes the helpless victim to a burrow, and lays a single egg. The wasp grub hatches and eats its way through the still-alive spider, then it changes into a pupa. It crawls out from the now-empty spider skin as a new adult.

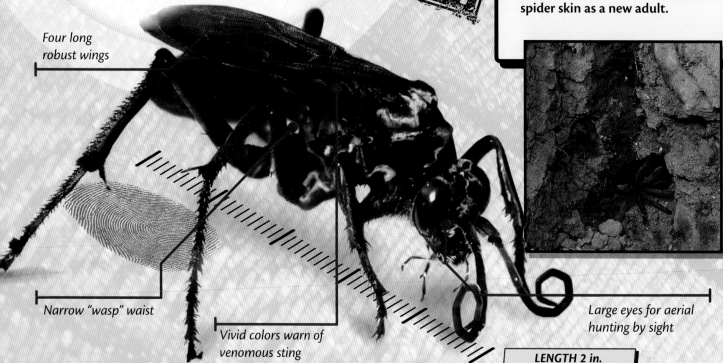

Four long robust wings

Narrow "wasp" waist

Vivid colors warn of venomous sting

Large eyes for aerial hunting by sight

LENGTH 2 in. (50 mm)

MEXICAN REDKNEE TARANTULA

Scientific name: *Brachypelma smithi*
How to say it: *Brack-ee-pell-mah smith-ee*

BATTLE FEATURES

DEADLY WEAPONS	8
SPEED AND AGILITY	8
BRUTE STRENGTH	9
BODY MASS	8
BRAINPOWER	6
ESCAPE ABILITY	7
TOTAL	**46**

Tarantulas and funnelwebs belong to the spider group known as **mygalomorphs**, or "**mouse shaped**," because of their chunky, hairy bodies. Their pair of sharp fangs point downwards, rather than at an angle or crossing like scissors. When threatened, tarantulas **rear up to show their fangs**, ready to jump forwards and thrust them down into enemy or prey.

CREATURE FEATURE

Large downward-pointing venom fangs. or chelicerae

Body covered with irritating hairs

Long muscular legs

LENGTH 4 in. (100 mm)
LEGS 6 in. (150 mm)

Eight eyes for good vision

Red Alert

For hours, the antlion larva waits, almost buried, at the bottom of its craterlike sand trap. The aim: to seize any bug that slips on the grains and tumbles down into its ferocious, pincerlike mouthparts. Red alert: a red fire ant appears on the crater rim. The lion hurls sand grains at it, the ant tumbles to its doom, and the larva impales the hapless victim, injecting its deadly toxin. But where there's one red fire ant, there are usually more. Suddenly, the lion is surrounded as the massed foes – named "fire" ants for a good reason – stab with their tail stingers, releasing a venom that causes intense burning pain.

RED FIRE ANT

Scientific name: *Solenopsis invicta*
How to say it: *Sow-len-op-siss in-vick-tah*

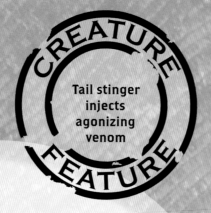

CREATURE FEATURE

Tail stinger injects agonizing venom

BATTLE FEATURES

DEADLY WEAPONS	7
SPEED AND AGILITY	7
BRUTE STRENGTH	5
BODY MASS	5
BRAINPOWER	6
ESCAPE ABILITY	6
TOTAL	**36**

As with termites, a single ant is no great problem – but dozens or hundreds can overwhelm an adversary. Fire ants belong to the same insect group as bees and wasps, the **hymenopterans**. As well as strong biting jaws, they have a **venom-injecting tail stinger**. If one ant is attacked, it releases an airborne **alarm scent**, a pheromone, that colony members quickly detect and follow, to help the troubled ant with a **mass attack**.

YOWL! HOT! HURTS!

Fire ants are named from the hot, burning pain caused by the stinger's venom. This hurts so much it can make a human howl in anguish. Imagine how it would feel to a small bug not much bigger than the ant!

Segmented antennae for finding the way and communicating in the colony

Long legs for fast movement

Sharp mandibles (jaws) that can slash and cut

LENGTH 0.1–0.3 in.
(3–7 mm)

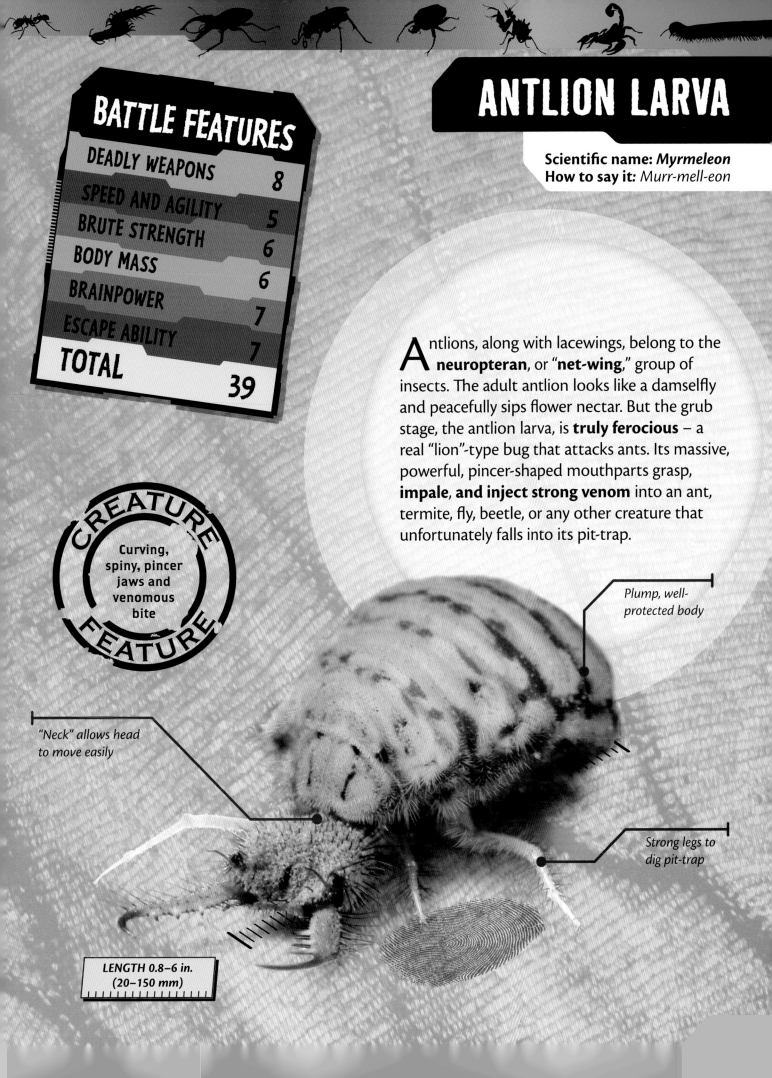

BATTLE FEATURES

DEADLY WEAPONS	8
SPEED AND AGILITY	5
BRUTE STRENGTH	6
BODY MASS	6
BRAINPOWER	7
ESCAPE ABILITY	7
TOTAL	**39**

ANTLION LARVA

Scientific name: *Myrmeleon*
How to say it: *Murr-mell-eon*

CREATURE FEATURE

Curving, spiny, pincer jaws and venomous bite

Antlions, along with lacewings, belong to the **neuropteran**, or "**net-wing**," group of insects. The adult antlion looks like a damselfly and peacefully sips flower nectar. But the grub stage, the antlion larva, is **truly ferocious** – a real "lion"-type bug that attacks ants. Its massive, powerful, pincer-shaped mouthparts grasp, **impale**, **and inject strong venom** into an ant, termite, fly, beetle, or any other creature that unfortunately falls into its pit-trap.

Plump, well-protected body

"Neck" allows head to move easily

Strong legs to dig pit-trap

**LENGTH 0.8–6 in.
(20–150 mm)**

Grappling Giants

Probably no one will die just yet – but these two massive monsters of the bug world can certainly deal out serious injury, which might later prove fatal. The megastick insect tried to remain unnoticed, courtesy of its stupendous camouflage. But the atlas moth has little to fear with its huge bulk and strength, hard-slapping, flapping wings, and stiff, irritant-chemical hairs. The megastick's spiky limbs kick violently to wound the moth as it sprays its noxious chemicals from its rear end. Quite possibly, after this colossal clash, both could perish.

ATLAS MOTH

Scientific name: *Attacus atlas*
How to say it: *At-ah-kuss at-lass*

Moths and butterflies make up the insect group called **lepidopterans**, or "**scale wings**," so named for the tiny scalelike units that cover their wings and give the colors and patterns. Despite its vast size, the atlas moth does not feed during its two weeks of adult life. Its mouthparts are not developed enough to take in nectar or similar foods. It lives on the nourishment stored when it was a hungry caterpillar.

WINGSPAN 10 in. (260 mm)

CREATURE FEATURE

Alarming snake's-head pattern on outer front wing

WONDER WINGS

The atlas is the world's biggest moth in terms of wing area, although not in its wingspan of 10–11 in. (260–270 mm). It lives in forests across South and Southeast Asia. Females are bigger than males.

Huge wings for forceful flight

Long feathery antennae

Body covered with irritant hairs

Gripping legs

BATTLE FEATURES

DEADLY WEAPONS	4
SPEED AND AGILITY	4
BRUTE STRENGTH	8
BODY MASS	9
BRAINPOWER	7
ESCAPE ABILITY	8
TOTAL	**40**

CHAN'S MEGASTICK

Scientific name: *Phobaeticus chani*
How to say it: *Foe-beet-ick-uss chan-ee*

FACT FLASH

Chan's megastick from Southeast Asia is the world's longest insect. Its head and body stretch 14 in. (350 mm), and with legs out straight in front, its total length is an astonishing 22 in. (570 mm)!

Stick insects, also called walking sticks or stick bugs, are in the insect group **Phasmatodea**, or "**ghost creatures**," containing over 3,000 species. Shaped and colored to look like old brown twigs, stick insects are among nature's finest examples of camouflage. In the rare cases they are noticed by a predator, stick insects may open their bright wings and flap away – or simply drop from their branch to the forest floor and scuttle off.

Brightly colored wings may flash when alarmed

Long thin antennae

Spiny legs for sturdy kick

CREATURE FEATURE

Amazing camouflage as a tree growth of sticks or twigs

BODY LENGTH 14 in. (350 mm)

Bullet Wounds

Wandering around, the bullet ant strays onto a colorful bloom. Wham! The flower mantis, almost invisible among the petals, whips out its jackknife front legs and clamps them onto the ant, spikes digging in to prevent escape. But even as the mantis chews the ant's antennae and eyes with its sharp, snipping mandibles, it suffers a searing pain, as though shot by a bullet. One of the ant's nest-mates has raced to the rescue in a frenzy of biting and stinging. Does the mantis yield up its prize meal and flee, or try to hold out against the bullet horde?

ORCHID MANTIS

Scientific name: *Hymenopus coronatus*
How to say it: *High-men-ope-uss koro-nah-tuss*

Mantises have their own insect group, **Mantodea** (see page 8). Many are well camouflaged, but the orchid mantis is one of the best, with a stunning resemblance to a safe-to-visit flower bloom. This mantis can even gradually change its color from brown to red to pink, all the better to lurk in and match, or **mimic**, its background of orchid petals.

BATTLE FEATURES

DEADLY WEAPONS	8
SPEED AND AGILITY	9
BRUTE STRENGTH	7
BODY MASS	7
BRAINPOWER	8
ESCAPE ABILITY	8
TOTAL	47

Big eyes to see all around

CREATURE FEATURE

Petal-like leg flaps for camouflage in a flower

Sharp mandibles slice up food

Folding front legs to snare victims

LENGTH 2.4 in. (60 mm) females
1 in.–1.2 in. (25–30 mm) males

BATTLE FEATURES

DEADLY WEAPONS	8
SPEED AND AGILITY	7
BRUTE STRENGTH	6
BODY MASS	6
BRAINPOWER	6
ESCAPE ABILITY	7
TOTAL	**40**

BULLET ANT

Scientific name: *Paraponera clavata*
How to say it: *Parra-pon-ear-ah klav-ah-tah*

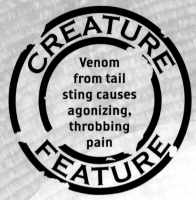

CREATURE FEATURE

Venom from tail sting causes agonizing, throbbing pain

LIKE A GUNSHOT

The bullet ant possesses one of the world's most feared stings. The venom causes terrible, almost unbearable, burning and throbbing pain that lasts 24 hours or more. Human victims say it's like being shot with a bullet – although hardly any of them had actually been shot!

Ants belong to the massive **Hymenoptera** insect group (see page 15). The bullet ant is one of **the world's biggest**, **strongest**, **and fastest ants**. Just one of them is a fierce foe, so several are an immense challenge for any bug. Bullet ants live in colonies of 200–500 and eat nectar, sap, and other plant juices, as well as preying on small creatures to bring back to the nest for their grubs.

Small hairs on body

Bent, or "elbowed," antennae

LENGTH 0.7–1.2 in. (18–30 mm)

Narrow waist between thorax and abdomen

Squelching Slayers

In the dripping wet forest undergrowth, a tiger leech loops along in search of blood to suck. Suddenly its way is barred by a hungry velvet worm prepared to fight for its feast. The leech scans its adversary with its ten eyes, readying its suckerlike toothed jaws that scrape and bore through almost anything. But the worm has a longer-distance weapon – it squirts disabling sticky slime at prey from openings on its head, then moves in to munch with jawlike mouthparts. The leech thrashes, trying to find a soft spot to suck into, but cannot squirm free of the worm's supersticky trap.

TIGER LEECH

Scientific name: *Haemadipsa picta*
How to say it: *Heem-ah-dip-sah pick-tah*

CREATURE FEATURE

Suckerlike toothed "jaws" at head end

BATTLE FEATURES

DEADLY WEAPONS	7
SPEED AND AGILITY	4
BRUTE STRENGTH	6
BODY MASS	7
BRAINPOWER	3
ESCAPE ABILITY	9
TOTAL	36

Ultimate bloodsuckers, leeches form a subgroup known as **hirudineans**, from an ancient word for **"worm-leeches."** They belong in the larger group **Annelida**, which includes earthworms, ragworms, lugworms, and many other worms. Leeches have a sucker at each end. Within the front sucker are **horny "teeth"** that bite and scrape through skin to get at blood and body fluids beneath.

GROSS!

Slimy, tough-skinned body

Squishy and flexible, able to squirm away from predators

Rear sucker holds on tenaciously

Nine-tenths of the weight of a recently fed leech is the blood inside it

**LENGTH 2 in.
(50 mm)**

VELVET WORM

Scientific name: *Peripatus*
How to say it: *Perry-pate-uss*

BATTLE FEATURES

DEADLY WEAPONS	7
SPEED AND AGILITY	7
BRUTE STRENGTH	7
BODY MASS	7
BRAINPOWER	7
ESCAPE ABILITY	7
TOTAL	42

CREATURE
FEATURE

Rows of stubby legs for fast movement

MISSING LINK?

Wormlike shape, more than a dozen pairs of caterpillar-style legs ending in claws, slime glands to spray sticky goo – the velvet worm is a real puzzle. And it's been around for perhaps 500 million years. Experts think it could be a missing link between legless worms and joint-legged arthropods such as insects.

Velvet worms are such unusual creatures that they have their own main group, **Onychophora**. It contains less than 200 species but it fascinates animal-lovers because velvet worms are a mix of several other main groups, such as worms, centipedes, and insects. They hunt at night and squirt small victims such as insects, snails, and spiders with a **gooey fluid** from the head end, which **traps the helpless victim**.

Head tentacles

Small simple eyes detect only light and shade

LENGTH 0.2–8 in.
(5–200 mm)

Stubby bendy legs

Titanic Face-off

There is a time for surprise – and a time for studying the opponent. These two megaheavy bugs display caution as they weigh each other up. In one corner the giant weta, in the other, the Goliath beetle. Neither has paralyzing venom or cutthroat jaws. But the weta boasts brutally gnawing mandibles and a disembowelling kick from its enormously powerful rear legs, while the beetle's bulk, head prong, and lashing foot claws may also deal deadly damage. Who will make that all-important initial charge...?

Crushing Clinch

With amazing speed, the monsters wrestle and grapple. Swiftly the beetle bulldozes under the weta's body and flicks it over, its cruel leg claws digging into the rival's abdomen. Caught off guard, the weta tries in vain to bite through the beetle's thick thorax shield with its strong mandibles. Then it struggles to bring its megakick into the fray, slipping and scratching the beetle's patterned wing covers with its spiny feet. Despite the weta's immense legwork, the hefty beetle manages to stay on top, as its fading foe slowly tires.

GIANT WETA

Scientific name: *Deinacrida*
How to say it: *Dane-ah-creed-ah*

BATTLE FEATURES

DEADLY WEAPONS	7
SPEED AND AGILITY	6
BRUTE STRENGTH	8
BODY MASS	8
BRAINPOWER	5
ESCAPE ABILITY	8
TOTAL	**42**

Wetas, with around 75 different species, are members of the grasshopper, cricket, and katydid group of insects, known as **orthopterans,** or "**straight wings**." Giant wetas are mainly plant-eaters and consume flowers, leaves, seeds, and fruits. But the **strong mandibles** needed to chomp tough food such as seeds mean they can tackle animal prey, too – and give a hefty bite in self-defense.

CREATURE FEATURE
Enormously powerful back legs for mighty kick

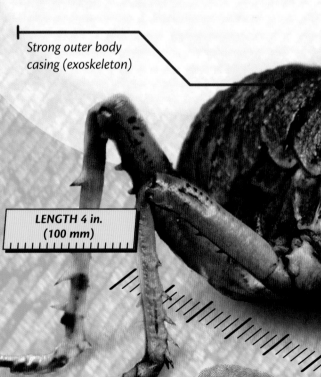

Strong outer body casing (exoskeleton)

Long sensitive antennae

LENGTH 4 in.
(100 mm)

Heavy, sturdy head and body

Robust mandibles (jaws) give penetrating bite

BATTLE FEATURES

DEADLY WEAPONS	7
SPEED AND AGILITY	6
BRUTE STRENGTH	9
BODY MASS	9
BRAINPOWER	7
ESCAPABILITY	6
TOTAL	**44**

GOLIATH BEETLE

Scientific name: *Goliathus*
How to say it: *Goal-eye-ah-thuss*

CREATURE FEATURE

Y-shaped bar on head for butting and lifting enemies

FACT FLASH

Both the giant weta and Goliath are true heavyweights of the bug world. The largest giant wetas tip the scales at 2–2.5 ounces (60–70 grams). The Goliath beetle is the official record-holder as heaviest of all insects – adults weigh 2 ounces (60 grams), but the grubs exceed 3.8 ounces (110 grams).

Beetles make up the vast **coleopteran** group of insects (see page 11). The Goliath beetle, named after the giant human of legends, is enormously heavy and **fantastically strong**. Yet its large rear wings, usually folded away neatly beneath the front wing covers, can lift this brute into the air. These beetles lead quiet lives sipping tree sap, flower nectar, and juicy fruits.

Patterned wing covers, or elytra

Patterned thorax (middle section of body with legs and wings)

LENGTH 4 in. (100 mm)

Sharp claws on long sturdy legs

Sensing Death

For a few seconds, it's a waiting game. The camel spider extends what look like its front legs, but they are hairy feelers, trying to evaluate the enemy. The giant vinegaroon flicks around its own sensor – its delicate tail-whip. The camel spider has magnificent fangs but no venom, while the vinegaroon snaps its imposing pincers in midair. Each opponent is so wary of a slashing blow to its main sensing part, will battle ever commence? In a shocking move, the vinegaroon spurts out its acid defense fluid. The camel spider dodges, and stand-off resumes. But not for long...

CAMEL SPIDER

Scientific name: *Solifugid*
How to say it: *Sol-ee-few-jid*

BATTLE FEATURES

DEADLY WEAPONS	8
SPEED AND AGILITY	8
BRUTE STRENGTH	8
BODY MASS	8
BRAINPOWER	7
ESCAPE ABILITY	8
TOTAL	47

Cousins of spiders and scorpions, in the main arachnid group, camel spiders have their own subgroup, called **solifugids** ("**fleeing from the sun**"). There are around 1,100 kinds and they have a host of other common names, such as wind scorpions and sun spiders. They seem to have five pairs of legs but the first pair are actually long, sensitive feelers called **pedipalps** that touch, smell, and taste their way around.

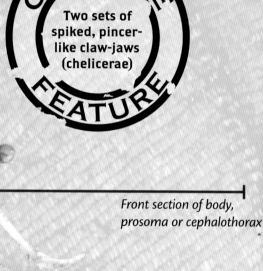

CREATURE FEATURE

Two sets of spiked, pincer-like claw-jaws (chelicerae)

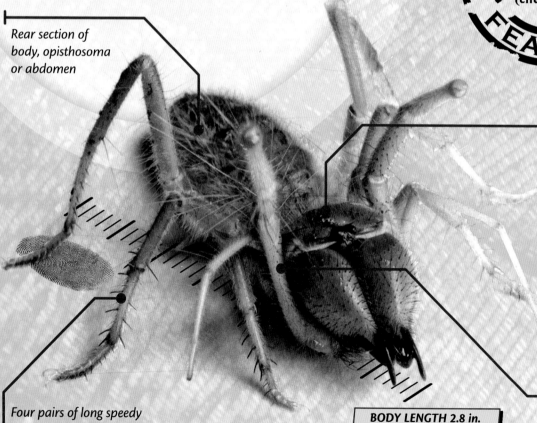

Rear section of body, opisthosoma or abdomen

Front section of body, prosoma or cephalothorax

Four pairs of long speedy legs for rapid running

BODY LENGTH 2.8 in. (70 mm)

Long pedipalps are very sensitive

BATTLE FEATURES

DEADLY WEAPONS	8
SPEED AND AGILITY	8
BRUTE STRENGTH	8
BODY MASS	8
BRAINPOWER	6
ESCAPE ABILITY	6
TOTAL	**44**

VINEGAROON

Scientific name: *Mastigoproctus giganteus*
How to say it: *Mass-tidge-owe-prock-tuss jie-gan-tee-uss*

CREATURE
FEATURE

Large, strong, spiny pincers to grasp victims

ACID ATTACK

The common name "vinegaroon" comes from the smell of the acid fluid this bug makes in glands in its abdomen. The fluid sprays from a hole at the rear end, underneath the base of the whip-like tail. It is mainly acetic acid – better known as vinegar!

Vinegaroons make up a small subgroup, **thelyphonids**, in the main arachnid group. Like their spider and scorpion relatives, they have four pairs of true legs – but no venom. And like scorpions, they possess powerful pincers, or pedipalps, to **seize and tear up** bugs, worms, slugs, spiders, and other small creatures for food. The long whiplike tail gives them another common nickname, **whip scorpion**.

Long whippy tail feels the surroundings

Front legs are very sensitive to touch and scents

Bases of front legs form squeezing vice to crush food

BODY LENGTH 3.3 in. (85 mm)

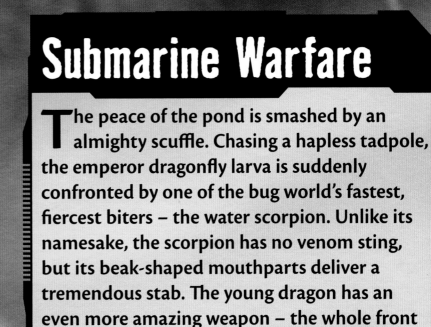

Submarine Warfare

The peace of the pond is smashed by an almighty scuffle. Chasing a hapless tadpole, the emperor dragonfly larva is suddenly confronted by one of the bug world's fastest, fiercest biters – the water scorpion. Unlike its namesake, the scorpion has no venom sting, but its beak-shaped mouthparts deliver a tremendous stab. The young dragon has an even more amazing weapon – the whole front of its face comes away like a death-dealing mask, to shoot forward and impale the enemy. The water scorpion counters with its clasp-knife, pinching front legs. Advantage sways one way, then the other...

EMPEROR DRAGONFLY NYMPH

Scientific name: *Anax imperator*
How to say it: *An-acks im-per-ah-tor*

Dragonflies and damselflies are superfast **aerial predators**, swooping on small flying creatures such as midges, gnats, mosquitoes, and small moths. They make up an insect group called **odonatans** ("**toothed**"), from toothlike spikes on their jaws. Just as fierce as the adult, the dragonfly nymph or young form (larva) lives in water and catches tadpoles, small fish, leeches, and water bugs with its extending "**head mask.**"

BATTLE FEATURES

DEADLY WEAPONS	9
SPEED AND AGILITY	7
BRUTE STRENGTH	8
BODY MASS	7
BRAINPOWER	6
ESCAPE ABILITY	5
TOTAL	**42**

CREATURE FEATURE

Hinged head mask shoots forward to grab victims

Beginnings of wings on back

Long legs for swimming and crawling underwater

Sharp mandibles (jaws) for cutting up prey

BODY LENGTH 0.4–2.8 in. (10–70 mm)

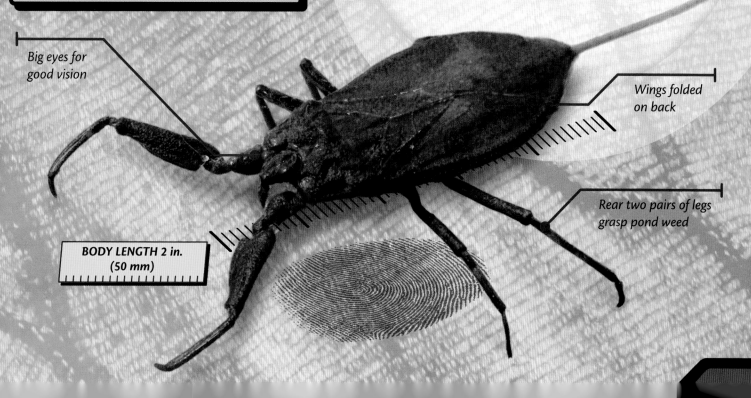

WATER SCORPION

Scientific name: *Nepa cinerea*
How to say it: *Nepp-ah sin-er-ee-ah*

BATTLE FEATURES

DEADLY WEAPONS	8
SPEED AND AGILITY	7
BRUTE STRENGTH	8
BODY MASS	7
BRAINPOWER	6
ESCAPE ABILITY	6
TOTAL	**42**

CREATURE FEATURE

Long, sharp-tipped, pincer-like front legs

SCUBA-SNORKELING SCORPION

Take a look at this photo – unlike a real scorpion, the water scorpion's long tail is not venomous. It is a long breathing tube, or snorkel, that brings fresh air down to an air bubble store, like a scuba tank, trapped between the lower surface of the bug's wings and its upper back.

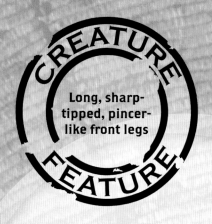

Water scorpions are in the **"true bug,"** or **hemipteran**, subgroup of insects (see page 30). The great, grabbing, clasp-knife pincers at the front end are in fact a pair of legs for grasping prey. The prey is then pulled close to the sharp, beaklike, **piercing mouthparts** typical of true bugs. The long tail works as an air tube, or snorkel, for breathing air.

Big eyes for good vision

Wings folded on back

Rear two pairs of legs grasp pond weed

BODY LENGTH 2 in. (50 mm)

Killer Wolf

A wolf pack attacks in numbers, but the beewolf is a lone killer. It flies in fast and slams its long, multi-use stinger into a worker honeybee or two, targeting between the front legs to disable a nerve center and render them paralyzed. Raid over, the beewolf carries the helpless prey to its nest as a banquet for its young. A couple of honeybees are powerless in the face of this rapid, savage offensive. But should the winged wolf delay by just a second, fellow hive workers rally and sting deep. The rear ends of the bees' bodies are torn off in the process, but their suicide mission safeguards the colony.

BEEWOLF

Scientific name: *Philanthus triangulum*
How to say it: *Fill-an-thuss try-ang-you-lum*

CREATURE FEATURE

Long stinger for venom can be used many times

BATTLE FEATURES

DEADLY WEAPONS	7
SPEED AND AGILITY	8
BRUTE STRENGTH	6
BODY MASS	6
BRAINPOWER	7
ESCAPE ABILITY	8
TOTAL	42

The beewolf is not a wolf, of course, or a bee. It's a wasp that hunts bees with the same dogged determination of a wolf chasing after prey. Wasps belong to the insect group **Hymenoptera** (page 40) and are fast, agile fliers. The beewolf targets several bees to sting, paralyze, and carry back to its nest burrow. Here its young grub will **feast on them**, one by one, until they are hardly-living husks.

GROSS!

Yellow and black warning colors

Huge eyes to hunt by sight

**BODY LENGTH 1.5 in.
(40 mm)**

Spiny lower legs

BATTLE FEATURES

DEADLY WEAPONS	7
SPEED AND AGILITY	6
BRUTE STRENGTH	5
BODY MASS	5
BRAINPOWER	5
ESCAPE ABILITY	5
TOTAL	**33**

HONEYBEE

Scientific name: *Apis mellifera*
How to say it: *Ay-pis mell-if-ur-ah*

CREATURE FEATURE

Barbed, venomous stinger, but one use only

MASS SUICIDE

Honey is such a fantastic source of energy and nutrients that many creatures, from small birds to massive bears, raid wild honeybee nests. The bees sting the raiders but then die. However, they are saving their nest-mates, who are all their sisters – so they give their lives for the family.

Like the beewolf, the honeybee is a **hymenopteran** insect. But while beewolfs are solitary, honeybees are **sociable**, living in big colonies and relying on each other for food, nest-building, and defense. Also, the bee's stinger has tiny **back-curved hooks**, or barbs, which means a once-only use – the barb stays in the victim as the bee flies away.

Like the beewolf, yellow and black colors warn off other insects

Big eyes to find food by sight

Pollen "basket" on rear leg

Hairy head and thorax

BODY LENGTH 0.2–0.6 in. (5–15 mm)

So, how did the bug battles play out? Sometimes the winner is clear-cut. Other contests went right to the wire. In most, a victor emerged – but perhaps so badly injured that it was unlikely to survive.

GIANT EARWIG VS. DEVIL'S COACH HORSE BEETLE

'WIG IS WINNER
Too fast for the lumbering beetle, the earwig nipped and gnashed it into submission.

BRAZILIAN WANDERING SPIDER VS. GIANT HORNET

STINGING TRIUMPH
The hornet's fast-buzzing wings and kicking legs allowed it to deliver a sudden sting to settle the bout.

SPINY FLOWER MANTIS VS. MADAGASCAR HISSING COCKROACH

BIG IS BEST
The 'roach's size, power, and surprising speed wore down the fast, plucky, but out-muscled mantis.

AFRICAN TERMITE VS. GIANT AFRICAN MILLIPEDE

TERMITES TERMINATED
The millipede's irritant defense fluid worked fast on the soft-bodied termites, securing its victory.

STAG BEETLE VS. GRAY SCORPION

VENOMOUS VICTOR
The stag beetle fought hard but was defeated by one stab of the stinger into its soft neck joint.

MASKED HUNTER ASSASSIN BUG VS. JUMPING SPIDER

SPIDER SLAYED
The masked assassin's combination of speed and stamina allowed it to land the last stabbing blow.

GIANT AMERICAN WATER BUG VS. MEGARIAN BANDED CENTIPEDE

CENTI SUCCESS
Fast, fierce multistrikes with its venom claws meant the centipede gradually paralyzed the water bug.

TARANTULA HAWK WASP VS. MEXICAN REDKNEE TARANTULA

WASP WINS OUTRIGHT
The wasp is superspecialized to hunt tarantulas and only tarantulas, and so was the favorite all along.

RED FIRE ANT VS. ANTLION LARVA

SEEING RED
The antlion's tough body casing repelled the worst of the ant stings as it burrowed to safety.

ATLAS MOTH VS. CHAN'S MEGASTICK

DEADLY DRAW
The two giant bugs pushed, shoved, flapped, and kicked so hard that neither lived to tell the tale.

ORCHID MANTIS VS. BULLET ANT

MIGHTY MANTIS
Quick as a flash, the mantis snipped and slashed the ants' antennae and eyes, rendering them helpless.

TIGER LEECH VS. VELVET WORM

WORM WINS WAR
The velvet worm's gummy spray proved the decisive factor in this war of the wrigglers.

GIANT WETA VS GOLIATH BEETLE

BEETLE BRAWN
Goliath's size and strength finally triumphed in this ultimate bug heavyweight contest.

CAMEL SPIDER VS. VINEGAROON

AGILE ASSASSIN
The camel spider's speed and agility allowed it to dodge the defense spray and deliver a lethal strike.

EMPEROR DRAGONFLY NYMPH VS. WATER SCORPION

PINCER MOVEMENT
The water scorpion's long stabbing pincer-legs proved decisive as they tore off the nymph's feeding "mask."

BEEWOLF VS. HONEYBEES

WOLF IS CONQUEROR
The beewolf cut its losses and managed to escape, swooping away with one honeybee victim.

Top Champion

Which bug would win the prize of overall champion? The megarian banded centipede seems to have it all – big and powerful, venom-stabbing, fanglike claws, sharp senses, tough body covering, and superlative speed on myriad legs with the ability to twist and dart like lightning. But if this bug had an off day – who knows?

MEGARIAN BANDED CENTIPEDE

Glossary

antennae
Long, slim, bendy, sensitive feelers on the head of many kinds of bugs, especially insects.

arachnids
Bug group whose adults have eight legs, including spiders, scorpions, camel spiders, mites, and ticks.

arthropods
Creatures with jointed legs, including insects, arachnids, centipedes, millipedes, and crustaceans.

blattodeans
The cockroach group of insects, which are mostly night-active and eat almost any foods.

carnivore
A predatory creature that hunts, kills, and eats other animals; a meat-eater.

chelicerae
Mouthparts of arachnids and related bug groups, which may be shaped like fangs, scissors, or crushers.

chilopods
The centipede bug group, with two legs per body segment and a pair of fanglike venomous claws, called forcipules.

coleopterans
The beetle group of insects, with the front pair of wings forming hard covers over the main body.

crustaceans
Arthropods that live mostly in water, such as crabs, lobsters, shrimps, prawns, and krill.

dermapterans
The earwig group of insects, scavengers that prefer dark damp places.

elytra
The hard, shieldlike front wings of beetles, which act as protection for the flying rear wings.

exoskeleton
The hard, tough, outer covering of many bugs, giving the body strength and shape.

forcipules
The front pair of legs of a centipede, specially shaped like sharp claws to deliver venom.

hemipteran
The "true bug" group of insects, with mouthparts, or rostrum, shaped like a sharp, stabbing beak.

hirudinean
The leech bug group, whose members are soft-bodied, with a sucker at each end.

hymenopterans
The insect group that includes ants, bees, wasps, and sawflies, which generally have a venomous sting.

isopteran
The termite group of insects, mostly soft, pale, and living underground; also called "white ants."

larva
The young form in the life cycle of many bugs, which hatches from the egg and feeds hungrily.

lepidopterans
The butterfly and moth group of insects, with four large wings covered in tiny mosaic-like scales.

lucanids
The stag beetle subgroup of beetles, in which the male's outsized jaws look like a stag's (male deer's) antlers.

lycosids
Wolf spiders, which run quickly after prey rather than spinning a web or similar traps.

mandibles
Mouthparts of insects and similar bugs, like jaws but moving side-to-side rather than up-and-down.

mantodeans
The mantis group of insects, with the front pair of legs shaped like grabbing shears or jackknives.

mygalomorphs
The spider group, including tarantulas, funnelwebs, and trapdoor spiders, with downward-pointing fangs.

neuropteran
The insect group that includes lacewings, mantis-flies, and antlions, with fierce, carnivorous larvae.

nymph
The young form in the life cycle of many bugs – a larva that looks similar in shape to the adult.

odonatans
The dragonfly and damselfly group of insects, which are underwater predators in their young stages.

onychophorans
Velvet worms, a curious group of bugs that have features of several others, and no close relatives.

orthopterans
The grasshopper, cricket, katydid, and weta group of insects, with very long powerful rear legs.

pedipalps
The long, sensitive feelers of spiders and similar arachnids; also the pincers of scorpions.

phasmatodea
The stick and leaf insect group, camouflaged to resemble twigs, buds, leaves, or flowers.

pheromones
Scents used by animals to send messages to others of their kind, in the air and spread on surfaces.

pupa
The third stage in the life of some insects and similar bugs, after the larva and before the adult.

rostrum
Long sharp mouthparts of true bugs (hemipterans), shaped like a bird's beak.

salticids
The jumping group of spiders, with large eyes for excellent vision and long leaping legs.

scorpiones
The scorpion group of arachnids, with large pincers, or pedipalps, and a venomous tail stinger.

solifugids
A group of arachnids with long legs, large fangs, but no venom or ability to spin silk.

spiracles
Breathing holes along the sides of the body in many bugs, which allow air in and out.

thelyphonids
The whip scorpion or vinegaroon group of arachnids, with pincers and a long whiplike tail.

tubercles
Lumps, bumps, or hornlike projections on the body of some bugs, especially on the head.

venom
Substance that causes pain, paralysis, or even death when injected by fangs or a stinger.

Index